D1417327

I Like Me

KIDS HAVE *TROUBLES* TOO

I Like Me

by Sheila Stewart and Rae Simons

Mason Crest Publishers

MASON CREST PUBLISHERS INC.
370 Reed Road
Broomall, Pennsylvania 19008
(866)MCP-BOOK (toll free)
www.masoncrest.com

First Printing
9 8 7 6 5 4 3 2 1

Library of Congress Cataloging-in-Publication Data
Stewart, Sheila, 1975–
I like me / by Sheila Stewart and Rae Simons.
      p. cm.
Includes index.
ISBN (set) 978-1-4222-1691-0   ISBN 978-1-4222-1699-6
ISBN (ppbk set) 978-1-4222-1904-1   ISBN 978-1-4222-1912-6 (pbk.)
  1. Self-esteem in children—Juvenile literature. 2. Self-esteem—Juvenile literature. I. Simons, Rae, 1957- II. Title.
BF723.S3S74 2011
155.4'182—dc22
                                         20100297220

Design by MK Bassett-Harvey.
Produced by Harding House Publishing Service, Inc.
www.hardinghousepages.com
Illustrations by Russell Richardson, RxDx Productions.
Cover design by Torque Advertising Design.
Printed in USA.

The creators of this book have made every effort to provide accurate information, but it should not be used as a substitute for the help and services of trained professionals.

Introduction

Each child is unique—and each child encounters a unique set of circumstances in life. Some of these circumstances are more challenging than others, and how a child copes with those challenges will depend in large part on the other resources in her life.

The issues children encounter cover a wide range. Some of these are common to almost all children, including threats to self-esteem, anger management, and learning to identify emotions. Others are more unique to individual families, but problems such as parental unemployment, a death in the family, or divorce and remarriage are common but traumatic events in many children's lives. Still others—like domestic abuse, alcoholism, and the incarceration of a family member—are unfortunately not uncommon in today's world.

Whatever problems a child encounters in life, understanding that he is not alone is a key component to helping him cope. These books, both their fiction and nonfiction elements, allow children to see that other children are in the same situations. The books make excellent tools for triggering conversation in a nonthreatening way. They will also promote understanding and compassion in children who may not be experiencing these issues themselves.

These books offer children important factual information—but perhaps more important, they offer hope.

—Cindy Croft, M.A., Ed., Director of the Center for Inclusive Child Care

I saw Samantha and Hailey as soon as I walked out onto the playground. They were standing over by the swings, and I was going to have to walk past them if I wanted to get to the tree where I liked to sit. Samantha and Hailey were the mean girls in the fourth grade. At least, they were mean to me.

I didn't even know why. They'd started picking on me almost as soon as school started this year, when I'd only lived in this town for a week.

I tried to walk around behind them to get to the tree, but they saw me anyway. Maybe they'd been watching for me.

"Oh, look," Hailey said. "It's Ava."

I'd never thought of my name as an insult before I'd met Samantha and Hailey.

"Are you going to go sit under that tree again?" Samantha asked. "I think the poor tree must be sick of seeing your stupid fat face."

I felt my face get hot, and tears collected in the corners of my eyes.

Hailey must have seen the tears. "What a baby!" she said. "Now she's crying!"

"She shouldn't even be in this class," Samantha said. "She should be in the baby class. Why don't you go back to China or Mexico or wherever you came from?"

"Where did you come from anyway?" Hailey asked. "You don't look like anything I've ever seen before."

Just walk away, I thought. I didn't want to be there anyway. I didn't want to sit under the tree anymore. I just wanted to go home. Since that wasn't possible, I turned around and walked in the other direction.

"Yeah, walk away!" Hailey yelled after me. "What a baby!"

"What a loser!" Samantha said. They both started laughing.

I walked back to the school and sat on the ground with my back against the building. Kids were running and laughing all over the playground. I wished I had a friend here. I missed my friends back home, in the city we lived in before we moved here. Nobody even tried to talk to me here. I didn't know what to do about it.

Later that day, we had gym. I used to be okay at gym. I mean, I wasn't the fastest runner or the strongest kid or anything like that, but I did fine and I wasn't terrible. That was at my old school, though. Now, I was terrible.

We were playing soccer in gym class. I actually liked soccer. It was one of the things I was best at. I liked running around and kicking the ball. Things started out badly this year, though. Maybe the problem was that I was shy. I got nervous when I saw all those kids I didn't know. Now, everybody thought I was the clumsiest kid that ever lived.

Mr. Hazel, the gym teacher, divided everyone up into two teams so we could play a game. Samantha and Hailey got put on different teams, and I was on Hailey's team.

"Oh no!" Hailey wailed. "Can't we switch Samantha and Ava, Mr. Hazel?"

"No," said Mr. Hazel.

Hailey stuck out her lip. "Now I'm going to lose. Ava always makes us lose."

It was probably even true, I realized. It didn't matter that I used to play fine at my old school, that I was even on a team; when Hailey and Samantha said I was terrible, I was just terrible. It was like they had some bad power over me.

Since we were playing in the gym, and we had a pretty big class, everybody couldn't play at the same time. Mr. Hazel liked to switch players out every once in a while. I hoped he would let me sit on the side for a while before I had to play, but he put me in the first group.

I was playing defense, which meant I didn't have to try to score goals on the other team, but it also meant I had to keep people from scoring on my team. I didn't do much for a while, because the ball was down at the other end of the gym. Then somebody from the other team got the ball and kicked it to Samantha, who was pretty close to where I was. I made myself run over and try to stop it from getting to her, but somehow I tripped. I didn't fall down, but I fell against Samantha. She shoved me away from her, and then I did fall down. I fell over the ball. My head cracked on the gym floor.

I didn't pass out, but I did just lay there with my eyes closed. I wished I had passed out. Then I wouldn't have heard everyone laughing, and I wouldn't have heard Samantha say, "What a loser," just like she had earlier.

By suppertime that night, I was miserable. I was tired of Samantha and Hailey, tired of this school, and tired of myself. Nothing was good anymore. I couldn't do anything right, I hated myself, and I wished I could just disappear.

Mom had made chicken tacos, which was one of my favorite meals, but I could hardly eat one bite.

Instead, I broke my taco shell into tiny pieces. I hoped no one would notice, but, of course, everyone did.

"Ava's not eating her food," Naomi, my little sister, said. "That means she can't get dessert, right?"

Naomi is four, and she's always getting yelled at because she doesn't want to eat supper but just wants cookies instead.

"I don't care," I said. "I don't want dessert anyway."

Mom put her hand on my forehead to see if I was sick, and Dad looked me straight in the eyes. "What's going on?" he asked.

I shrugged. "I don't know," I said—which, of course, was a lie. "I guess I just had a rough day at school."

"Is it those girls again?" Mom asked.

"What girls?" I didn't remember telling Mom about Samantha and Hailey.

"You said last week that some girls in your class were being a little mean to you?"

I'd forgotten I'd even said that much. Mom and Dad and Naomi all looked at me. I didn't know what to say. I stared down at my plate and squeezed my taco harder and harder. The shell crunched into lots of pieces, and the pointy bits poked my fingers. Everything started getting blurry as my eyes filled up with tears.

"Honey?" Dad put his hand on my arm. "Tell us what's going on."

I didn't say anything for a minute, but everything got blurrier and blurrier. My throat was burning and choking me.

"I hate school," I finally said. "I hate everything about it. I hate myself. I'm ugly and stupid and clumsy, and everybody else hates me too."

Nobody said anything at first, and the tears that had been filling up my eyes overflowed and ran down my face. I figured they all knew I was right and were surprised I was just figuring out how terrible I really was.

"Why did you say you're ugly?" Naomi asked. "You're beautiful."

"Everybody makes fun of me," I said. "Samantha and Hailey mostly. They said they don't know what I am but I'm ugly. And they said I'm stupid and a loser and a baby."

I looked over at Mom. She looked really, really mad. I thought at first she was mad at me, but then she said, "Those little brats! I'd like to have a few words with them!"

Mom has bright red hair, and she always says she has a temper to match. I don't know what that means exactly, but Dad, who is half Mexican and half Japanese, is a lot calmer most of the time.

"Come here," Dad said. He reached over and took hold of my hand, then pulled me up from chair and over to where he was sitting. Then, even though I was nine years old, he pulled me into his lap and wrapped his arms around me, like he used to when I was little.

"Those things aren't true," Dad said. "You are not ugly. You are not stupid. You are not any clumsier than anyone else. Those girls were very, very wrong to say those things to you. It is never okay for people to bully you. You are beautiful—just like Naomi said. You are intelligent. I know you're not clumsy all the time because I've been to your soccer games before we moved. And even if those things were true—which they're not—it would not be okay for anyone to be cruel to you. Ava, darling, you have so many amazing and wonderful things about you."

I put my head on Dad's shoulder. "Am I fat?" I asked.

"No," he said. "You are a perfectly normal weight for your height."

"They said they wanted me to go back to wherever I came from but they didn't know where that was because they'd never seen anything like me."

"Well, it's true that you have a very mixed-up background," Dad said, "with ancestors from all different places. But you should know that most people think that makes you more interesting."

"I wish I looked like Mom." I pulled on my dark hair. "Mom's beautiful. No offense," I added, looking up at Dad, because I have his dark hair and dark eyes.

"None taken," Dad said. "I agree that Mom is beautiful. But there is more than one kind of beautiful. I happen to think you're gorgeous. In the long run though, it doesn't matter what Samantha and Hailey think about you; it only matters what you think about you."

"I hate myself," I said immediately.

"But that's only because you've been listening to the wrong people. Bullies like to make themselves feel good by making other people feel bad. They like thinking they have power over you."

"Some people are just mean," Mom said, "and you can't change that."

"You can only control what you do and think, not what other people do and think," Dad added. "Those girls think they can control you, but that's only because you've been letting them. You can't stop them from being mean, but you can find ways of dealing with it."

"Like what?" I asked.

"Tell your teacher!" shouted Naomi. "She'll fix it."

"No way," I said, but Mom said, "Naomi's right. Your teacher needs to know about what's going on." She stood up and walked out of the kitchen.

"What about the other kids in your class?" Dad asked. "Maybe some of them would be better friends for you."

"No, they all hate me," I said.

"All of them? I really don't think so. They probably just don't know anything about you. Listen," he said, "I have an assignment for you. Two assignments really. First, next time Samantha and Hailey start being mean to you, you stand up straight, look them in the eyes, and then turn around and walk away. Go and tell the teacher what's happening. Second assignment is to pay attention to the other kids around you. Maybe somebody else is looking for a friend."

Naomi started crawling into Dad's lap, too, and he pulled her up to sit on his other leg. The two of us hugged him, and I smiled for the first time in what seemed like a long time.

After a few minutes, Mom came back into the kitchen. "I just talked to Mrs. York," she said.

"What?" I asked. Mrs. York was my teacher. "Mom! Why?"

"Because she needed to know what was going on. She said she'll keep an eye on those girls and deal with them if she notices them bullying you."

"I think that might just make things worse," I said.

"It might," she said, "but probably not."

I wasn't sure that was very encouraging.

The next morning on the bus, I thought about what Dad had said, about paying attention to the other kids. I looked at the kids sitting around me. The boy in front of me had headphones on and was staring out the window. The girl in the seat across from me was talking to the girl behind her. They didn't look mean, but they didn't look like they needed a friend. And I didn't really want to make a friend, because I didn't know how. I just wanted to have a friend.

The bus stopped, and a couple more kids got on. We had assigned seats on the bus, and one of the kids who got on was the girl who sat with me. I didn't even know what her name was, but I thought she was in one of the other fourth grade classes. I'd never paid much attention to her, but now I looked at her. She had a round face and curly brown hair. She sat down and pulled out a book, like she always did, but the bus jerked and it slipped out of her hand. Normally, I would have been staring out the window and pretending I wasn't there, but since I was already looking at her, it felt rude to ignore her book. I reached down and picked it up and handed it to her.

"Thanks," she said and smiled at me.

I smiled too, but then I got nervous and looked out the window again.

I got through the first part of day without much trouble. In class, all I had to do was listen to Mrs. York and do the work. But then we had recess, which is when things were usually worst.

Out on the playground, I looked over at my tree. I had really liked just sitting under it and day-dreaming. But, just like yesterday, Samantha and

Hailey were standing over there. I sighed and sat down with my back against the school again.

I was watching a few of the kids play basketball, and I didn't even notice when Samantha and Hailey showed up and stood over me.

"Are you hiding, Ava?" Hailey asked.

I looked up and wished I hadn't. Everything Dad had said went through my mind for one second, but I felt frozen. I wished I was standing up, so I could look them in the eyes. They seemed so much bigger than I was this way.

I tried to stand up, but they were standing too close to me.

"Move," I said, but my voice wasn't working very well.

"What?" Samantha asked. "Did you say something, loser?"

"I said move!" I tried to get to my feet.

Samantha shoved me, and I fell back onto the ground. "Don't even think about it," she said.

For some reason, I heard Dad's voice in the back of my head, saying, "It is never okay for people to bully you." And I got mad. I was so tired of being miserable and hating myself.

"What is your problem?" I yelled at Samantha. "What did I ever do to you?" I looked her in the eyes, like Dad had said, even though it was hard because I was still sitting on the ground and she was standing up. You would have thought that Samantha and Hailey would be so shocked I had stood up for myself they would have left me alone, but that didn't happen.

Instead, they started laughing. It was like they had won some kind of contest by making me mad.

I wanted to cry again, but just then, two things happened at the same time. The first thing was that somebody said, "Hey, do you need help?" And the second thing was Mrs. York's voice, saying, "Samantha and Hailey! Leave Ava alone and come with me right now!"

The second thing surprised me, because I hadn't really thought Mrs. York would do anything, even though Mom had called her, but the first thing totally shocked me. I couldn't quite believe somebody had actually been talking to me, but when Samantha and Hailey stepped away, I looked up and saw the girl who sat next to me on the bus. She was holding out her hand to help me stand up.

After a second, I took her hand and let her pull me up. "Thanks," I said.

"You're Ava, right?" she said. "I'm Juliette."

"Hi, Juliette."

The next day, I asked Mom if Juliette could come over sometime. We started being friends, and it wasn't as hard as I'd thought. Samantha and Hailey started picking on me less, too. It wasn't like everything was perfect, but it was better.

A couple of weeks later, Juliette slept over at my house, and Mom and Dad let us stay up late to

watch a movie. We laughed so hard we kept falling over.

"You're so funny, Ava," Juliette said. "I never would have guessed that about you!"

I was surprised, because I would never have guessed it about me, either. I was so glad Juliette and I had become friends. I thought about hating myself and thinking everything was so awful. Sometimes, I still worried that Samantha and Hailey had been right. "No," I told myself. "They weren't right. They were bullies. I might not be perfect, but I am not a loser."

I grinned at Juliette. "You know what?"

"What?"

"I like you, Juliette. And you know what else?"

Juliette grinned back at me. "What?"

"I like me."

Liking Yourself

Sometimes it feels like everyone around you is judging you, including yourself. How pretty or handsome are you? Did you get good grades? Have you traveled out of the country? Can you sing? Do you weigh too much or too little? The answers to these questions and others like them can seem pretty important. Even as kids, everyone has to worry about whether or not other people like them. Equally important is whether or not you like yourself.

How you feel about yourself is called self-esteem. Esteem means thinking that something is important or valuable, and self means you, as an individual person. You either have high or low self-esteem, depending on how much you like yourself. If you're confident, respect yourself, and like who you are, then you have high self-esteem. On the other hand, if you don't like who you are, and are constantly putting yourself down, then you have low self-esteem.

How well liked you are by other people, and how well liked you are by yourself are related. If you have low self-esteem, then other people can often tell and might take advantage of that fact and make fun of

This girl probably has high self-esteem, since she's happy with her reflection in the mirror.

you. If you have high self-esteem, then others will notice all those good things about you and will treat you well.

What Self-Esteem Is Not

Self-esteem simply means that you think you're important. It doesn't mean that you tell the world how great you are—that's called bragging. In fact, people who brag about themselves often have low self-esteem. They're trying to convince everybody else how great they are by telling them about a trophy they won or all the places they've been in the world. They're also trying to convince themselves at the same time.

Self-esteem is also about accepting your flaws. Nobody's perfect, so no one expects you to be either. Everyone has flaws and things they can't do well. That shouldn't change your self-esteem, though. You're still a valuable person even if you aren't the fastest runner or don't get the best grades in math. If you truly have high self-esteem, then you'll accept your flaws and work on the ones you want to fix.

Growing Self-Esteem

People aren't really born with self-esteem. They grow it. Babies don't like or dislike themselves when they're born, because they're too busy worrying about getting fed and exploring the world. As we get older, though, we become more **self-aware**. We realize that we are individual people, with different abilities and different characteristics. We also realize that some people don't like us, and others do.

By the time we're in elementary school, we start to have a sense of self-esteem. It's based on our achievements so far, how many friends we have, and how our families interact. For example, if your parents have encouraged you to do things you're good at and have told you how proud of you they are, then there's a good chance that you feel good about who you are. On the other hand, if kids at school are mean to you, or if things at home aren't the best, then you might end up with low self-esteem. It doesn't really have anything to do with whether you're

> ## *Understand the Word*
>
> When you realize that you're a person with thoughts and beliefs, you are **self-aware.** People don't become self-aware until after they're babies.

a good person or not. It has to do more with how you grew up.

High Self-Esteem

People with high self-esteem are confident and like who they are. They still have good and bad days, and they get upset when they don't do things well, but they still value themselves. People with high self-esteem usually:

Winning medals or trophies boosts your self-esteem, since they offer proof that you can do something well.

- Take pride in what they do. They might really enjoy playing an instrument, and work hard to play it the best they can. They might be nervous before a concert, but they also want to show their family and friends what they've accomplished.
- Try new things. Running for class president sounds scary, for example, but kids with high self-esteem might try it anyway. Even if they lose, at least they had a new experience. If they win, then they're confident that they can handle the responsibility.
- Act independently. They know they can do things, or at least give it their best. They aren't afraid to do things by themselves because they trust themselves and know that they can rely on themselves.

Understand the Word

Optimism is the tendency to always think that things will turn out for the best. Someone is optimistic if she looks on the bright side, if she thinks the "glass is half full." The opposite of optimism is pessimism.

People with high self-esteem still have problems, but they can deal with them more easily and have that extra confidence and **optimism** that makes them happier.

Low Self-Esteem

People with low self-esteem don't have confidence in themselves and feel that they're not valuable. At first, Ava had low self-esteem when she moved to her new school. Her thoughts and actions are typical of a kid with low self-esteem. People who suffer from low self-esteem might:

- Put themselves down. They tell themselves that they aren't good at anything, and that any successes they have are just luck. Putting yourself down includes telling yourself you're ugly, that you're no good at anything, or that no one cares about you.
- Avoid trying new things. It's not worth it for people with low self-esteem to try new things, since they think they'll just be bad at them anyway.
- Take the blame for everything. Even if something is not his fault, someone with low self-esteem might accept responsibility for it. If everything else is his fault, then why not this, too? For example, if a boy fails all his spelling tests, and then his friend does too, then he might blame himself for not helping his friend study more.

- Let themselves be bullied. They don't have enough self-confidence to tell others to stop making fun of them or bullying them. They might not really believe what the bullies say, but it still takes higher self-esteem than they have to stand up to them.
- Think negative thoughts. They spend a lot of time thinking about how bad their lives are, and how nothing good ever happens to them. They don't focus on all of the good parts of their lives.

Low self-esteem makes you unhappy. Fortunately, there's no reason you have to have low self-esteem. There are lots of ways to improve how you feel about yourself, and you'll be happier in no time.

Body Image

Body image is how you think of your physical body. There's a lot of pressure to look just right—you can't be too fat, you can't be too short, you can't be too plain-looking. Maybe someone has made fun of you for how you look, like how Samantha and Hailey made fun of Ava for looking different.

Remember, attractiveness means different things for different people. We don't all have to look like movie stars, and in fact, most of us don't. Take a look around, and you'll see all sorts of different sized and shaped people. You don't want to be unhealthy, but you should also learn to be okay with how you look. A lot of self-esteem is tied to how we think we look, so the sooner you like how you look, the sooner you'll like how you are.

Understand the Word

The effects of actions are called **consequences**. The consequence of dropping a plate on the floor, for example, is that the plate breaks.

Why Do I Have Low Self-Esteem?

Many, many people don't like themselves, for lots of different reasons. Ava used to like herself fine, when she had lots of friends and enjoyed playing soccer. But then she moved to a new town, where she didn't know anyone, and her self-esteem dropped. Moving is such a big change, no wonder it had such big **consequences**.

School can cause your self-esteem to get worse. If you're struggling to get good grades and understand the material, then you might start thinking you're stupid. Or even if you were happy with your grades, but all your friends did better, you might feel that you aren't keeping up with them.

Self-esteem has a lot to do with how we feel about our appearance. This boy is concerned about his weight, which might lower his self-esteem.

Big life events can also cause your self-esteem to drop. Moving and not making friends right away, your parents' divorce, or **puberty** could make you think differently about yourself, and make you like yourself a little less.

You Are Who You Are

The first step to gaining high self-esteem is to accept yourself for who you are. That's much easier said then done, but once you do that, then you're well on your way to higher self-esteem.

If you're constantly worrying about your big feet or about how bad you are at basketball, then it'll be much harder to like yourself. First, you have to concentrate on being okay with how you are, including your body, your abilities, and your feelings. You have to come to terms with the fact that you can't change certain things about yourself, and it's useless to worry about changing them. You'll never get anywhere if you only focus on what you can't change.

The Next Steps

Okay, so you want higher self-esteem, and you've started accepting who you are. Now what? High self-esteem doesn't just appear over night; you have to work at it for a while before it becomes natural. For now, focus on all the things you're good at instead of all the things you're bad at. Make a list of everything you think you can do well. Include talents like singing or drawing, but also list things like telling a good joke, listening to people who need to talk, or taking care of your pets. You'll probably be surprised at how much stuff is on there that you never thought about before.

Keep focusing on all those things even after you make the list. When you notice that you've done something well during the day, make sure you tell yourself. You'll still feel bad about the things you don't do well, but if you point out the things you actually do well, then you'll start to change your **mindset**.

Understand the Word

A **mindset** is a fixed way of thinking about things. A person whose mindset is that she is ugly will always feel bad about her appearance, regardless of how nice she may really look.

Keeping a list of everything you like about yourself might be hard to start, but it'll help you see that you're an amazing person!

If you're worried about your body, then you might consider going to the doctor. Don't go if you just don't like your hair color, or if you wish you had more (or fewer) freckles. However, if you're worried about being too fat or too thin, then talking to your doctor might be a good idea. Otherwise, focus on the positive, like you're already doing. Your body is pretty cool, if you take the time to think about it. Tell yourself how strong your arms are when you swim, not how bad you think you look in a swimsuit.

The Reward

Ava figured out that by being more self-confident and refusing to believe that she was worthless, she gained a friend. If you can learn how to raise your self-esteem, you'll be happier—and you may make new friends too. It takes some work, but the reward is worth it in the long run. Maybe you'll make a new friend if you have the courage to talk to someone new, or you'll be able to raise your grades, or you'll discover that you're really good at art. You deserve to enjoy your life—and yourself!

Questions to Think About

1. How do people who don't like themselves act differently from people who do like themselves?

2. Do you like yourself? Do you ACT like you like yourself?

3. Why do you think Ava started having so many problems with her self-esteem?

4. What do you think will happen to Ava next, now that her attitude has started to change and she likes herself better?

Further Reading

Adams, Christine. *Happy to Be Me.* St. Meinrad, Ill.: Abbey Press, 2001.

Covey, Sean. *Just the Way I Am.* New York: Simon & Schuster, 2009.

Covey, Sean. *The Seven Habits of Happy Kids.* New York: Simon & Schuster, 2008.

Kaufen, Gershen. *Stick Up for Yourself: Every Kid's Guide to Personal Power & Positive Self-Esteem.* New York: Free Spirit, 2000.

Find Out More on the Internet

Feeling Good About Yourself
www.cyh.com/HealthTopics/HealthTopicDetailsKids.
aspx?p=335&np=287&id=1588

Self-Esteem
www.buzzle.com/articles/self-esteem-activities-for-kids.html

The Story on Self-Esteem
kidshealth.org/kid/feeling/emotion/self_esteem.html

The websites listed on this page were active at the time of publication. The publisher is not responsible for websites that have changed their address or discontinued operation since the date of publication. The publisher will review and update the websites upon each reprint.

Index

Picture Credits

AZPWorldwide; fotolia: p. 31
Coburn, Stephen; fotolia: p. 38
Wicklund, Jaren; fotolia: p. 42
Wierink, Ivonne; fotolia: p. 34

To the best knowledge of the publisher, all images not specifically credited are in the public domain. If any image has been inadvertently uncredited, please notify Harding House Publishing Service, 220 Front Street, Vestal, New York 13850, so that credit can be given in future printings.

About the Authors

Sheila Stewart has written several dozen books for young people, both fiction and nonfiction, although she especially enjoys writing fiction. She has a master's degree in English and now works as a writer and editor. She lives with her two children in a house overflowing with books, in the Southern Tier of New York State.

Rae Simons is a freelance author who has written numerous educational books for children and young adults. She also has degrees in psychology and special education, and she has worked with children encountering a range of troubles in their lives.

About the Consultant

Cindy Croft, M.A. Ed., is Director of the Center for Inclusive Child Care, a state-funded program with support from the McKnight Foundation, that creates, promotes, and supports pathways to successful inclusive care for all children. Its goal is inclusion and retention of children with disabilities and behavioral challenges in community child care settings. Cindy Croft is also on the faculty at Concordia University, where she teaches courses on young children with special needs and the emotional growth of young children. She is the author of several books, including *The Six Keys: Strategies for Promoting Children's Mental Health.*